# ALLAH IS GOD

Published by Ali Gator Productions 2021, First Edition
Copyright © 2021 Author: Yasmin Nordien
First Published 2021

National Library of Australia Cataloguing–in-Publication (CIP) data:
Allah is God
Author: Yasmin Nordien, Illustrator: Maryann Jaraisy
ISBN: 978-1-921772-72-6
For primary school age, Juvenile fiction

**T:** +61 (3) 9386 2771
P.O. Box 2536, Regent West, Melbourne Victoria, 3072 Australia
**E:** info@ali-gator.com **W:** www.ali-gator.com

*In the name of God,*
*Infinitely Compassionate, Most Merciful.*

# ALLAH IS GOD

*By yasmin nordien*

**This book is for my beloved parents,**
**Amina Albertus (Nordien) and Nasser Nordien al Aqrabi; my husband and our son.**

As a child, my parents taught me, what their parents taught them, and their parents taught them - *'Islam is a simple way of life'* 'hold on tight to the rope of God' with trust. The poems are my attempt to capture what I was taught, and to pass it to my son and future generations.

*To my beloved children Dana and Amir,* who inspire me with their playfulness
and make every ordinary shine in speciality.
mary ann jaraisy

# Content

## Allah is God

Allah is God.
God is One.
Like God, there is none.

Creator of all things, big and small.
God is God, and that is all.

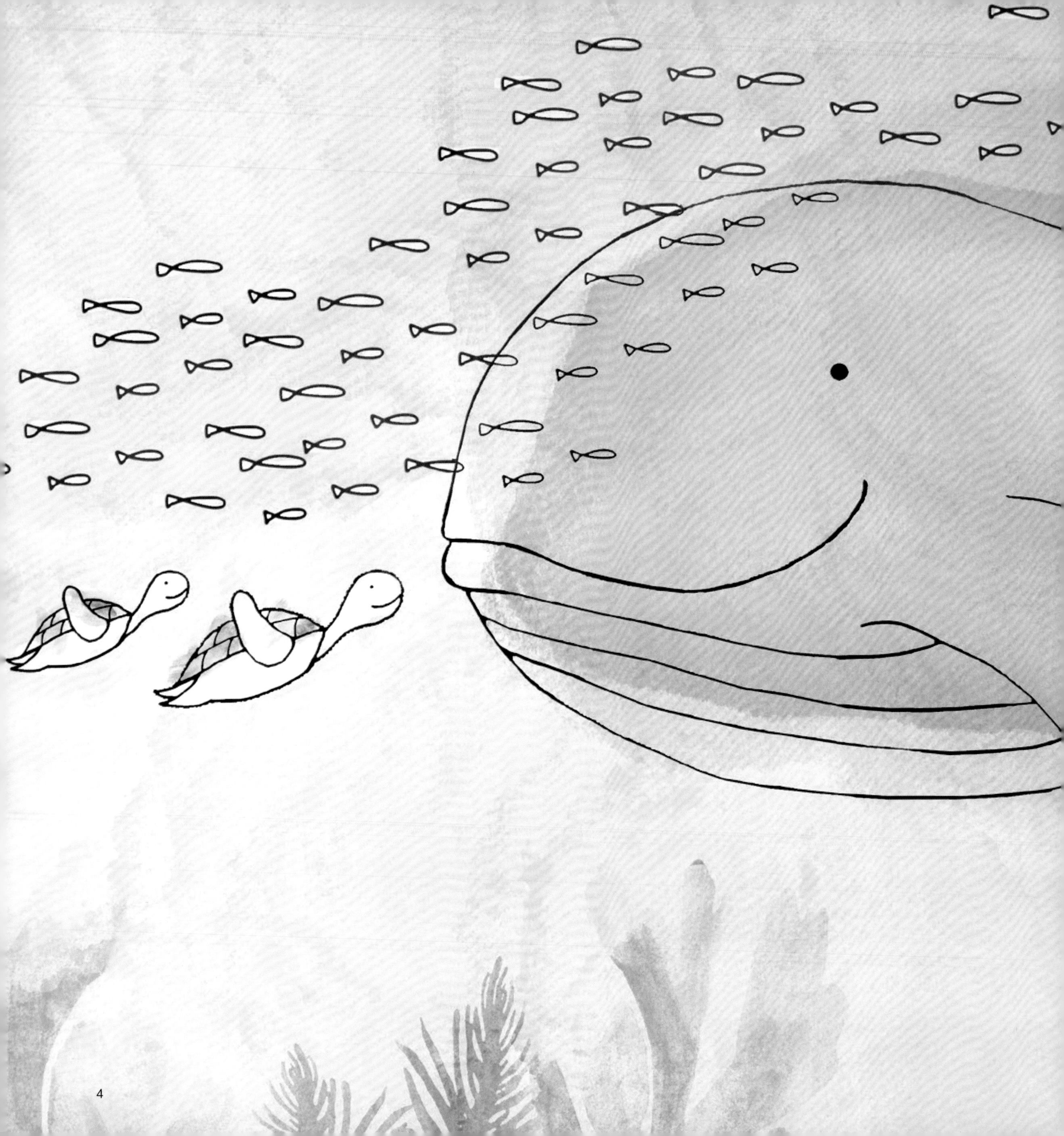

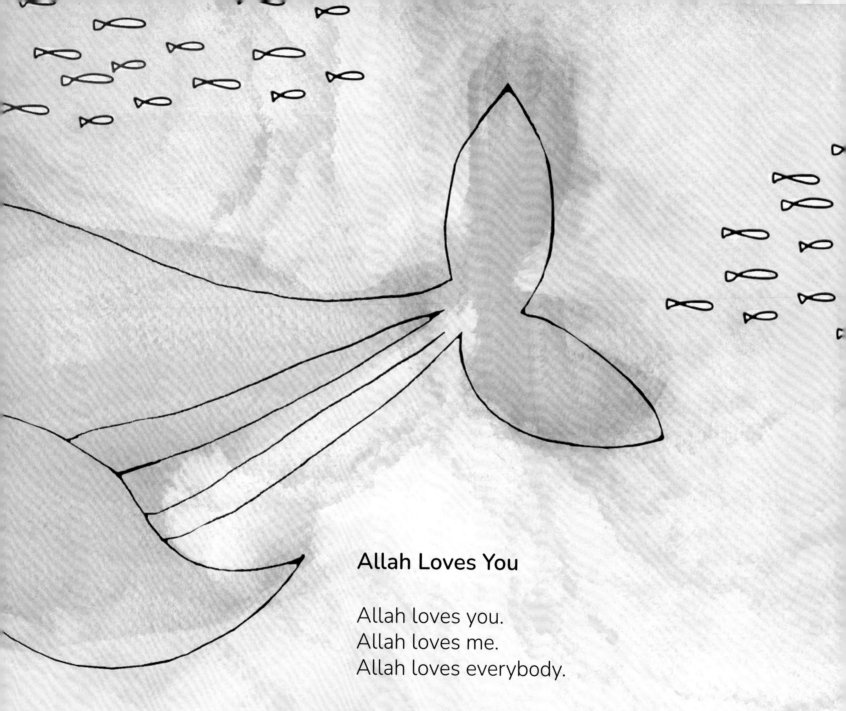

**Allah Loves You**

Allah loves you.
Allah loves me.
Allah loves everybody.

La ilaha illallah, there is no God but God.

Allah is here.

Allah is there.

**Allah is Everywhere.**

La ilaha illallah, there is no God but God.

## From God, To God

Where do I come from?
From God.
Where am I going?
To God.

From God we come, to God we return.
Inna lillahi wa inna ilayhi raji'oon.

## Allah Knows

Allah knows everything, Al-Alim.
Allah sees everything, Al-Basir.
Allah hears everything, As-Sami.

Allah knows, sees and hears everything.
La ilaha illallah, there is no God but God.

## Allah Made Me, ME!

Allah made me, ME!
Allah made my body, fingers, and toes
and put on my cute button nose.

Allah coloured me in -
chocolate brown, candy pink, and colours in between.
All yummy colours you must agree, God chose for me.

Allah made me, ME!
And as you can see, I am as beautiful as can be.
Unique and perfect, as Allah intends me to be.

I AM BEAUTIFUL ME!

Alhamdulillah, All Praise to Allah.

## Allah Made Everything

Allah made you.
Allah made me.
Allah made everybody.

Allah made flowers.
Allah made trees.
Allah made animals, birds and bees.

Allah made the earth.
Allah made the sea.
Allah made the universe and planets for all to
look and see.

Allah made day.
Allah made night.
Allah threw in the sun, moon and stars to
bring light.

Allah Hu Akbar, God is Great.

## He or She

He or She,
What God be?

Allah is not like you and me.
God is more than our eyes can see, beyond he and she.

God be what God Be.
God is God, like you are you and I am me.

## Allah is One

Allah is Unique.
God is One.
Like Allah, there is none.

Allah is Infinite.
God is Great.
Allah has no body, size or shape.

Allah is Love.
God is Life.
Allah performs miracles in a trice.

Allah is Perfect.
God is Wise.
Allah knows what we need before we decide.

Allah is Just.
God is Fair.
Allah loves those who do good and care.

Allah is Truth.
God is Light.
In following guidance, we are alright.

Allah is Love.
God is One.
Allah's breathe is in everyone.

La ilaha illallah, there is no God but God.

## Be!

Allah said, Kun Faya Kun!
BE! and it IS.

Be!
And bang,
Creation came into being.

Be!
The universe and worlds explode into existence.
Planets, suns, and moons burst forth.

Be!
Angels, jinn and humans are formed.
All of creation is called into existence.

God names a thing, and it flowers into being.
Kun Faya Kun! BE! and it IS.

## Dying to Meet God

Inna lillahi wa inna ilayhi raji'oon.
From God we come, To God we return.

Between coming and going,
we pass through two doors. Birth and Death.

Born to know and worship God.
Striving, walking a straight path back to God.

And death, death is the doorway back to God.
We die to be with God, again.

## Ask Allah

Allah is Love.
God cares.
When you're hurt, ask for help and Allah is there.

Allah protects you.
God guides.
When you're in trouble and don't know what to do;
call for help, God will come through.

Allah is Merciful.
God is Kind.
When you are naughty and not very nice;
ask sincerely, Allah forgives without thinking twice.

Allah is Giving.
God provides.
When you're in need and don't know what to do;
call on God to help you.

Allah is Omniscient.
God hears and answers all prayers.
Trust in Allah, and the answer will come to you.

Allah is Omnipotent.
God is Everywhere.
When you're feeling scared and all alone, call Allah Hu.
God is always with you.

Call Allah in thanks, Call Allah in crisis.
Call just to say, 'dear God you are the nicest!'

Omniscient means all-seeing, all-knowing, wise.
Omnipotent means all-mighty, all-powerful, invincible, unstoppable, supreme.

# The Backstory

The poems were co-created with my son, and written over a few years, in response to questions and conversations we had.

**Allah is God.  Allah Loves You.  God is Everywhere.  Allah Knows.  Allah Made Everything**
These poems were written to introduce him to God, when he was a little boy.

**Allah is One.**  As he got older, we discussed who is God? and what is God?

**He or She?**  One day he asked me 'is God a boy or a girl?'

**From God, to God.**  My mother died, and he asked *'where is ouma Amina?'* I responded with the age old response of Muslims *'we come from God, and we go back to God'*, his response was *'oh, okay'* and he continued playing.

**Allah Made Me, ME!** He started becoming aware of differences; in particular how he is different (allergies, gender, race, religion, abilities, etc.).  The poem sought to teach him a core Islamic value, to value and celebrate diversity; and to be okay with being different. (Quran 49:13)

**Be!**  One day he shared what he had learnt in school about creation
(theory of evolution). The poem is a response, based on verses in the Quran
which speaks about creation. (Quran 2:117 and 3:47)

**Dying to Meet God.**  Death visited us again and again - the family dog died, a friend's mom died, our son heard the story of how his cousin died in childhood, and our neigbhour died. The poem is about the life-death cycle.

**Ask Allah.** The poem is an attempt to give him comfort and solace in difficult situations.